AF270124

MIRACLE MOMENTS & THE HISTORY OF SPORTS

BOOKS OUT LOUD COLLECTION

MIRACLE MOMENTS & THE HISTORY OF SPORTS

KENNY ABDO

BOOKS OUT LOUD

BLACK STONE PUBLISHING

ABDO

Welcome to BOOKS OUT LOUD!
This one-of-a-kind collection consists
of twelve wildly popular Abdo Zoom titles,
the bestselling classroom favorites. Get ready
to feed your brain with the same amazing Abdo
Read-to-Me experience kids know and love
at school—and become a powerhouse reader
anytime, anywhere.

Please scan the QR code on the back cover to
link to the accompanying audio, or visit
www.Downpour.com/miracle-moments-in-sports

Published in 2024 by Blackstone Publishing

Printed in the United States of America

978-8-212-53823-7
Juvenile Nonfiction / Sports & Recreation / General

Version 1

Blackstone Publishing
31 Mistletoe Rd.
Ashland, OR 97520

www.BlackstonePublishing.com

Contents

MIRACLE MOMENTS IN
BASEBALL

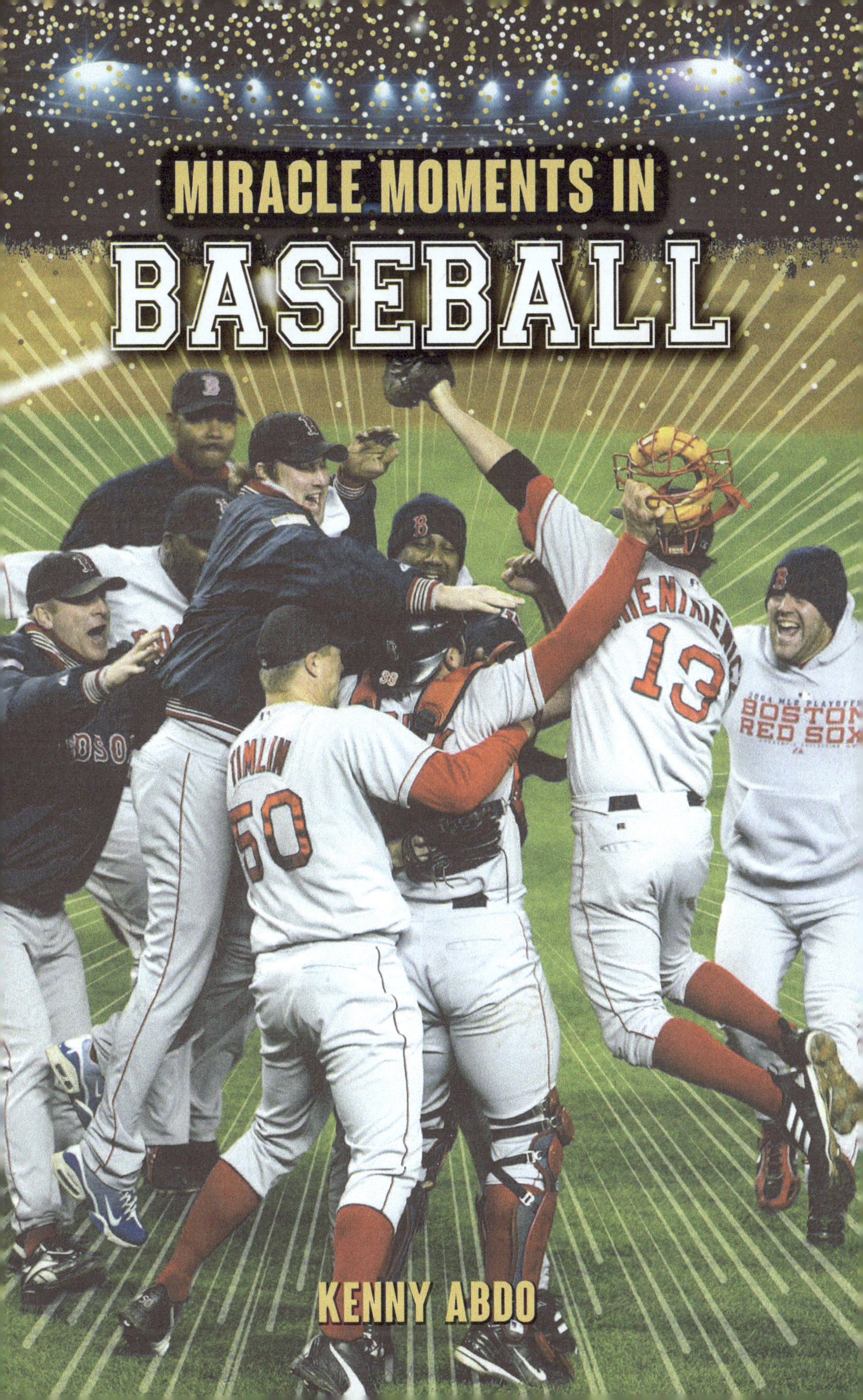

KENNY ABDO

TABLE OF CONTENTS

BASEBALL

Rightly called America's "national **pastime**," baseball is one of the most popular sports in the world!

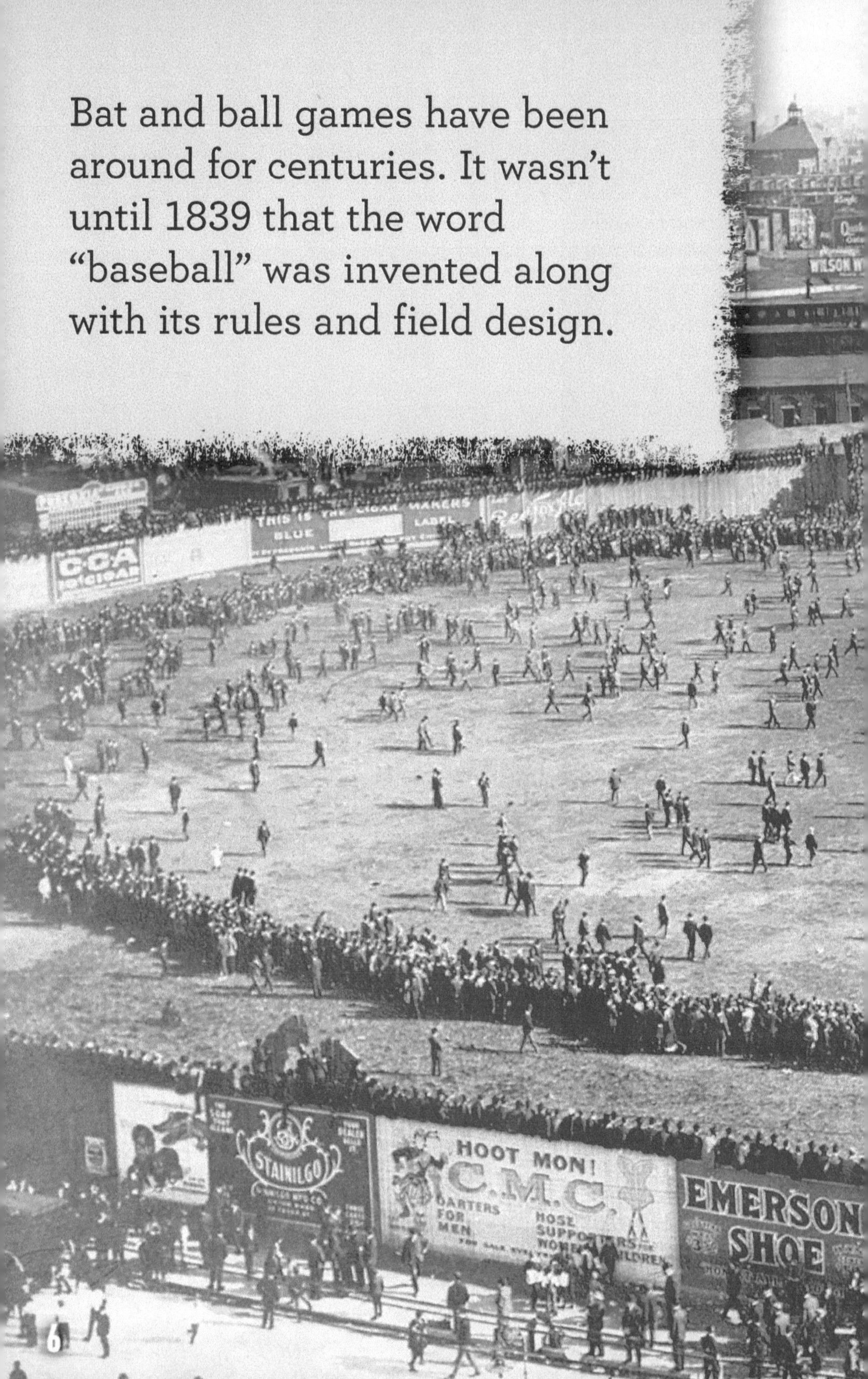

Bat and ball games have been around for centuries. It wasn't until 1839 that the word "baseball" was invented along with its rules and field design.

Omega
FORCE
Royal
HUNTINGTON
AVENUE
AMERICAN LEAGUE
BASE BALL
GROUNDS

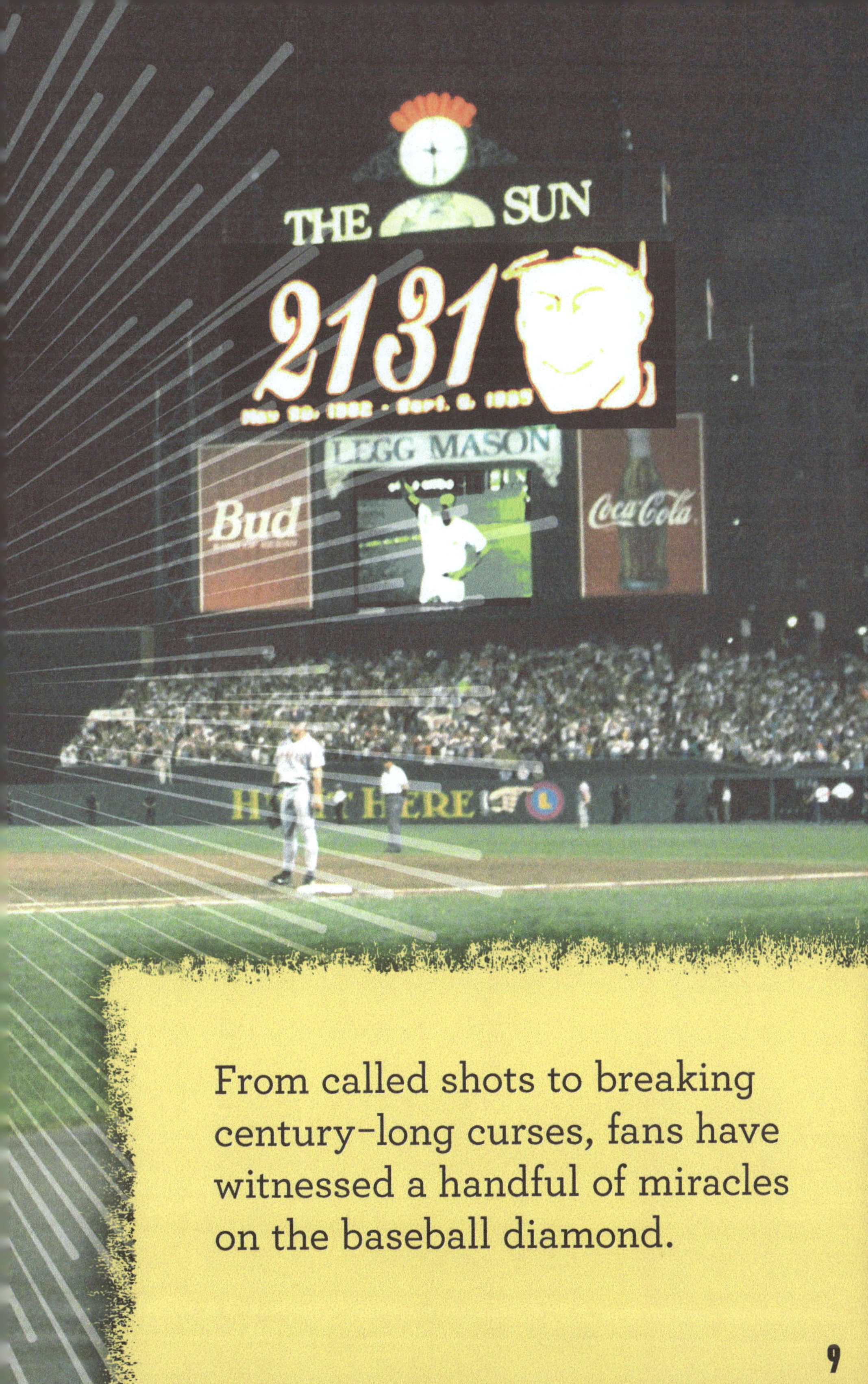

From called shots to breaking century-long curses, fans have witnessed a handful of miracles on the baseball diamond.

DO YOU BELIEVE?

In 1932, Babe Ruth pointed with his arm toward the center-field bleachers at Wrigley Field. He slammed the ball in that exact direction into a crowd of 50,000 crazed fans. The Yankees went on to win 7 to 5.

The Giants needed a miracle to secure the **pennant** against the Dodgers in 1951. In the bottom of the ninth of a tied game, Bobby Thomson hit a home run **clinching** the win. It was called the "Shot Heard 'Round the World."

Mickey Mantle pulled a muscle in his left forearm during a 1961 game against the Detroit Tigers. At risk of being **benched**, he said his arm was fine. Holding the bat with just his right fist, he launched the ball for his 49th and 50th home run of the **season** that game. The Yankees won a three game **sweep**.

The Atlanta Braves led the 1991 **World Series** against the Minnesota Twins. Kirby Puckett was 3-for-18 hits the entire series. In the bottom of the 11th inning of a grueling tied game 6, Puckett finally hit a homer. The Twins won the World Series the next night!

Twins
34

The Red Sox won the 2004 **World Series** for the first time since 1918 to break the **Curse of the Bambino**. The Sox did it again, sweeping the Rockies in 2007. They **clinched** more victories in 2013 and 2018, assuring fans that the first win wasn't just a fluke.

LEGACY

Baseball miracles have captured the imagination of audiences in every medium. From books to movies like *61**, *The Sandlot*, and *Field of Dreams*. *Fever Pitch* crews had to quickly rewrite the end of the movie because of the Red Sox's unexpected 2004 victory.

For almost 200 years, baseball miracles have made an already beloved sport even more wonderous to its fans.

GLOSSARY

benched – taking a player out of the game for a certain amount of time.

clinch – to confirm a win.

Curse of the Bambino – an 80-year period of not winning the World Series for the Boston Red Sox after they traded Babe "Bambino" Ruth in 1918.

pastime – an activity people participate in for their enjoyment.

pennant – a flag representing a sports championship.

season – the portion of the year where certain games are played.

sweep – winning a series of games without any losses.

World Series – a yearly series of games, where the team who wins a best-of-seven playoff is determined the champions of the year.

MIRACLE MOMENTS IN
BASKETBALL
KENNY ABDO

TABLE OF CONTENTS

BASKETBALL

From driveways to packed arenas, basketball boxes out all other sports!

On a rainy day in 1891, Canadian gym teacher James Naismith looked for a way to keep his class busy. He found a peach basket and had the students toss a ball into it for points.

Buzzer beaters and untouchable records are some of the miracles that have changed basketball forever.

JIM BEAM
BOURBON & BURGERS
THIS WAY
108
109
OUBRE JR.
3
MORRIS
11
NUGGETS
5

DO YOU BELIEVE?

Magic Johnson was 20 years old during game 6 of the 1980 **Finals**. He scored 42 points, had seven assists, and handled 15 rebounds. That was unheard of for a **rookie**. Johnson led the Lakers to win the NBA **title** that year.

NATIONAL BASKETBALL
ASSOCIATION
AND
SPORT MAGAZINE'S
MOST VALUABLE PLAYER AWARD
1980
WORLD CHAMPIONSHIP
SERIES

In 1986, Ralph Sampson hit one of the luckiest shots in NBA history. With a tied score and one second left on the clock, Sampson caught the ball and hit the **layup**, winning the game for the Rockets.

Michael Jordan finished his Bulls career strongly with the final shot he made for the team. Down by one point, Jordan made a deciding shot over Bryon Russell with just seven seconds to go. They won, making it Jordan's sixth and last **Finals** victory.

In 2009, Kobe Bryant hit a miracle **buzzer beater** from behind the arc. The incredible shot won the game for the Lakers, beating the Heat by a close 108–107.

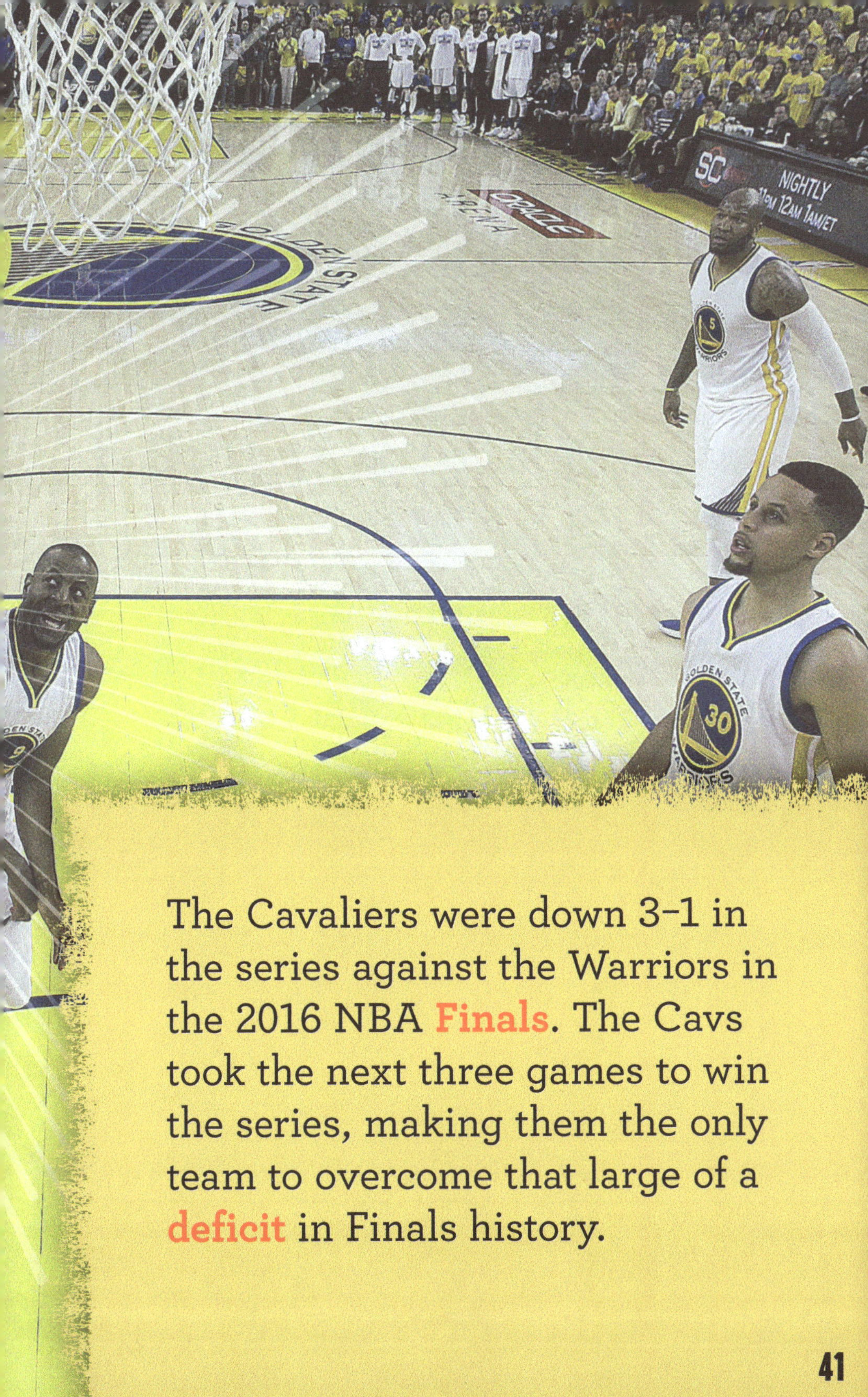

The Cavaliers were down 3-1 in the series against the Warriors in the 2016 NBA **Finals**. The Cavs took the next three games to win the series, making them the only team to overcome that large of a **deficit** in Finals history.

LEGACY

Most basketball miracles are preserved in books and highlight reels. ESPN's *30 for 30* series focused on NC State coach Jim Valvano's winning nine do-or-die games in a row. Seven of which the team was losing in the final minute.

Basketball has come a long way from peach baskets. But what hasn't changed is the possibility of witnessing miracles on the court.

GLOSSARY

buzzer beater – a shot scored at the very last second of a basketball quarter.

deficit – the amount of points that a team is losing by.

do-or-die – when the only two options are success or failure.

Finals – the championship series of the NBA where the team who wins best-of-seven games is determined champions of the year.

layup – a onehanded shot made from right under the basket.

rookie – an athlete during their first full season of their sport.

title – a first-place position in a contest.

MIRACLE MOMENTS IN
FOOTBALL
KENNY ABDO

Photo Credits: Alamy, AP Images, Icon Sportswire, iStock, Newscom,
North Wind Picture Archives, Shutterstock
Production Contributors: Kenny Abdo, Jennie Forsberg, Grace Hansen
Design Contributors: Dorothy Toth, Neil Klinepier

TABLE OF CONTENTS

FOOTBALL

Going long for more than
100 years, football is a sport
hardcore fans cheer for!

The National Football **League** (NFL) was formed in 1920. It was just 10 teams from four states that created the American Professional Football Association (APFA). It was renamed the NFL in 1922.

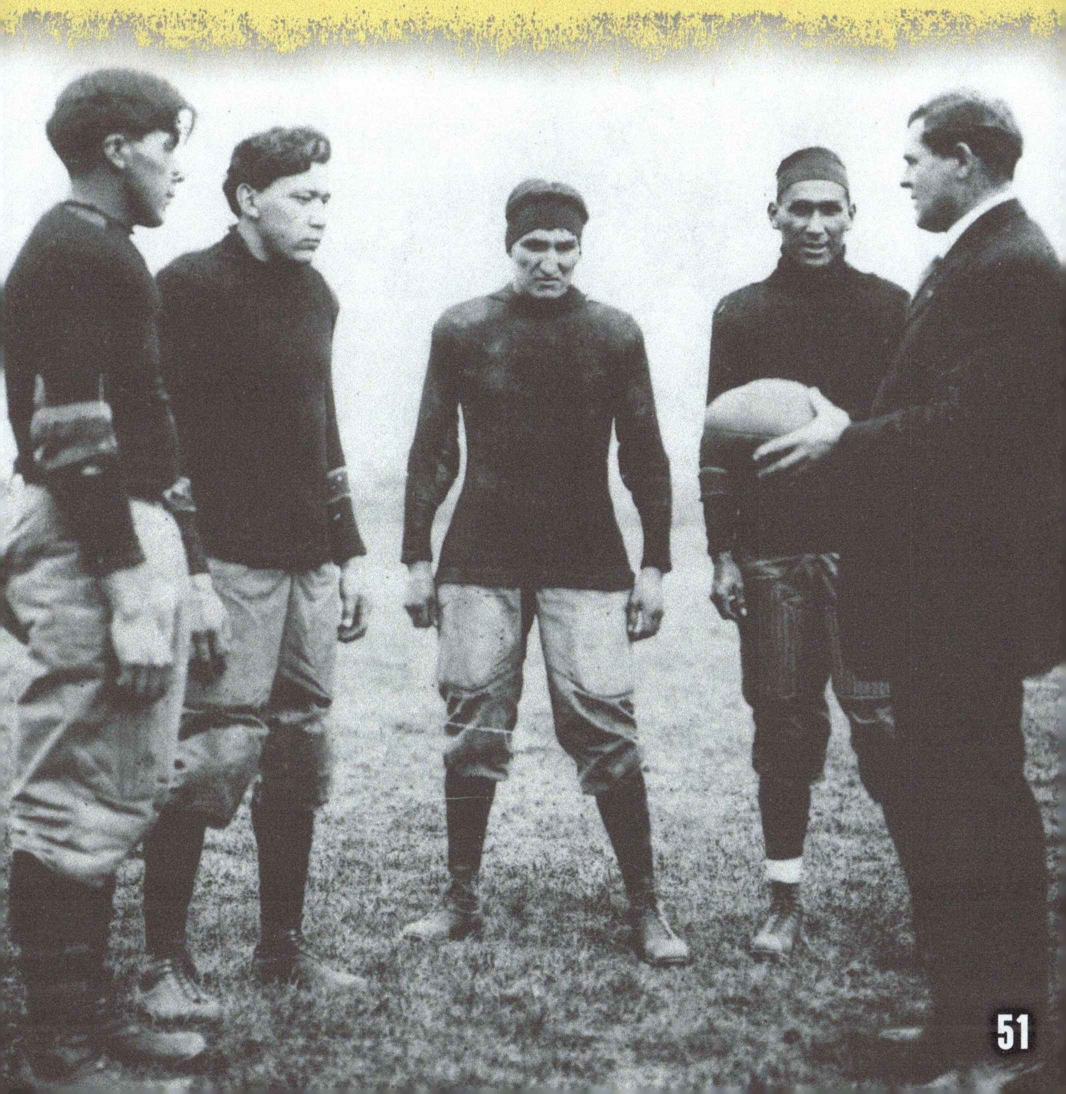

Since the beginning of pro football, fans have witnessed several miracles on the gridiron, sometimes with the help of a Hail Mary.

DO YOU BELIEVE?

The Eagles trailed the Giants by five points in a 1978 game. A fumble was recovered by Herman Edwards. He ran the ball 26 yards for a winning touchdown! It was named the Miracle at Meadowlands.

In 1982, the 49ers were down six points with one minute to go. Joe Montana had to throw the ball away to avoid getting **sacked**. Dwight Clark leapt into the air, catching the wild ball above his head. He scored the winning touchdown in that **NFC Championship**!

E.JONES
72
16
88

On January 3, 1993, the Bills were down 35-3 in the third quarter against the Oilers.

The Bills scored an unbelievable 35 **unanswered** points in the fourth quarter. They won the game! It was the largest comeback in NFL history.

With 10 seconds left in the 2018 divisional playoff game, Stefon Diggs caught a pass from **QB** Case Keenum, and ran 61-yards for a touchdown. The Vikings beat the Saints 29-24 with the play known as the Minneapolis Miracle.

Trailing by 5 points with 7 seconds to go on December 9, 2018, the Dolphins completed two **lateral passes** leaving **running back** Kenyan Drake with the ball. Drake ran 52 yards to solidify the Miami Miracle!

LEGACY

Football's greatest miracles have made it on **highlight reels**, showcasing the greatness every team can achieve.

Whether it is catching the uncatchable or running impossible distances, football inspires every generation to go for the extra point!

GLOSSARY

highlight reel – the best moments of a certain game or athlete compiled into one film.

lateral pass – when the ball carrier passes to a teammate behind him.

league – a group of teams that compete against each other.

NFC Championship – the annual championship of the National Football Conference.

quarterback (QB) – the player on the offensive team that directs teammates in their play.

running back – an offensive player who specifically carries the ball.

sacked – when a quarterback is tackled behind the line of scrimmage while still in possession of the ball.

unanswered – when one team scores many points without the other team scoring.

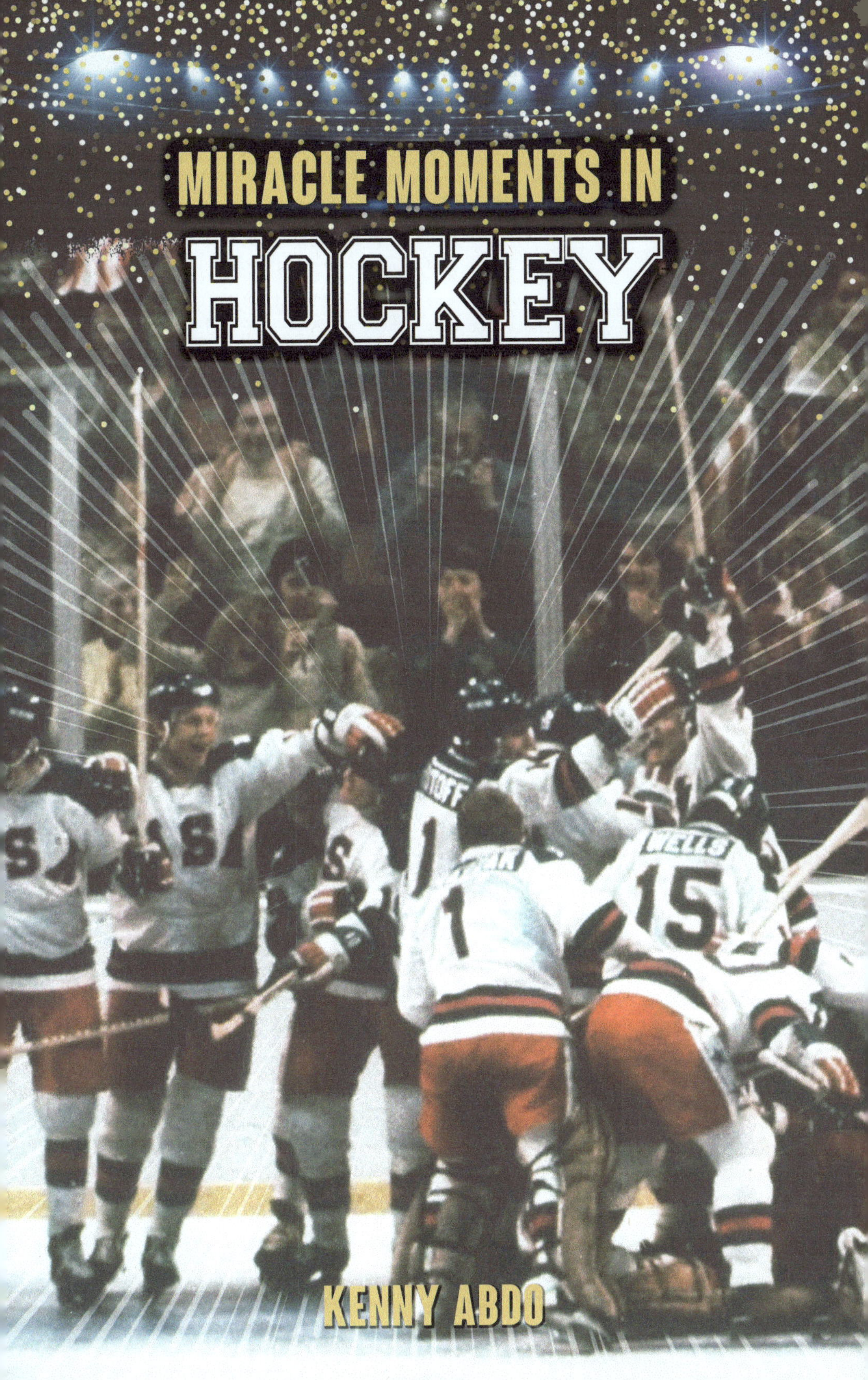

MIRACLE MOMENTS IN
HOCKEY
KENNY ABDO

Photo Credits: AP Images, Everett Collection, Granger Collection, Icon Sportswire, iStock, Newscom, Shutterstock
Production Contributors: Kenny Abdo, Jennie Forsberg, Grace Hansen
Design Contributors: Dorothy Toth, Neil Klinepier

TABLE OF CONTENTS

HOCKEY

From North America to the Czech Republic, hockey makes an ice-cold sport red hot with excitement.

Curved stick and ball games can be traced back 4,000 years to Egypt. Canada takes ownership of putting it on ice late in the 19th **century**.

In that time, miracles ranging from **barn burners** to broken-legged shots have etched themselves into hockey history.

DO YOU BELIEVE?

In 1964, Maple Leafs Bob Baun left the ice in Game 6 of the **Stanley Cup**. He had broken a leg. Baun returned to the game in **overtime playoffs**. He scored the game-winning goal. The team went on to win the Stanley Cup.

During the 1980 Winter Olympics, the less-experienced Team USA beat the indestructible **Soviets**. It is known as the "Miracle on Ice."

The final score was 4-3, leading to announcer Al Michael's iconic final call, "Do you believe in miracles?!"

The Capitals and Islanders
performed their own Easter
Sunday miracle in 1987. The
game started at 7:30 PM on
Saturday night and ended
at 1:58 AM. It is the longest
Game 7 in **Stanley Cup playoff**
history. The Islanders won the
Easter Epic.

Blackhawks Patrick Kane broke a 49-year curse in 2010. He scored the winning goal against the Flyers in **overtime**. Nobody saw the shot go in because of the angle. "Phantom goal" or not, the Blackhawks won the **Stanley Cup**!

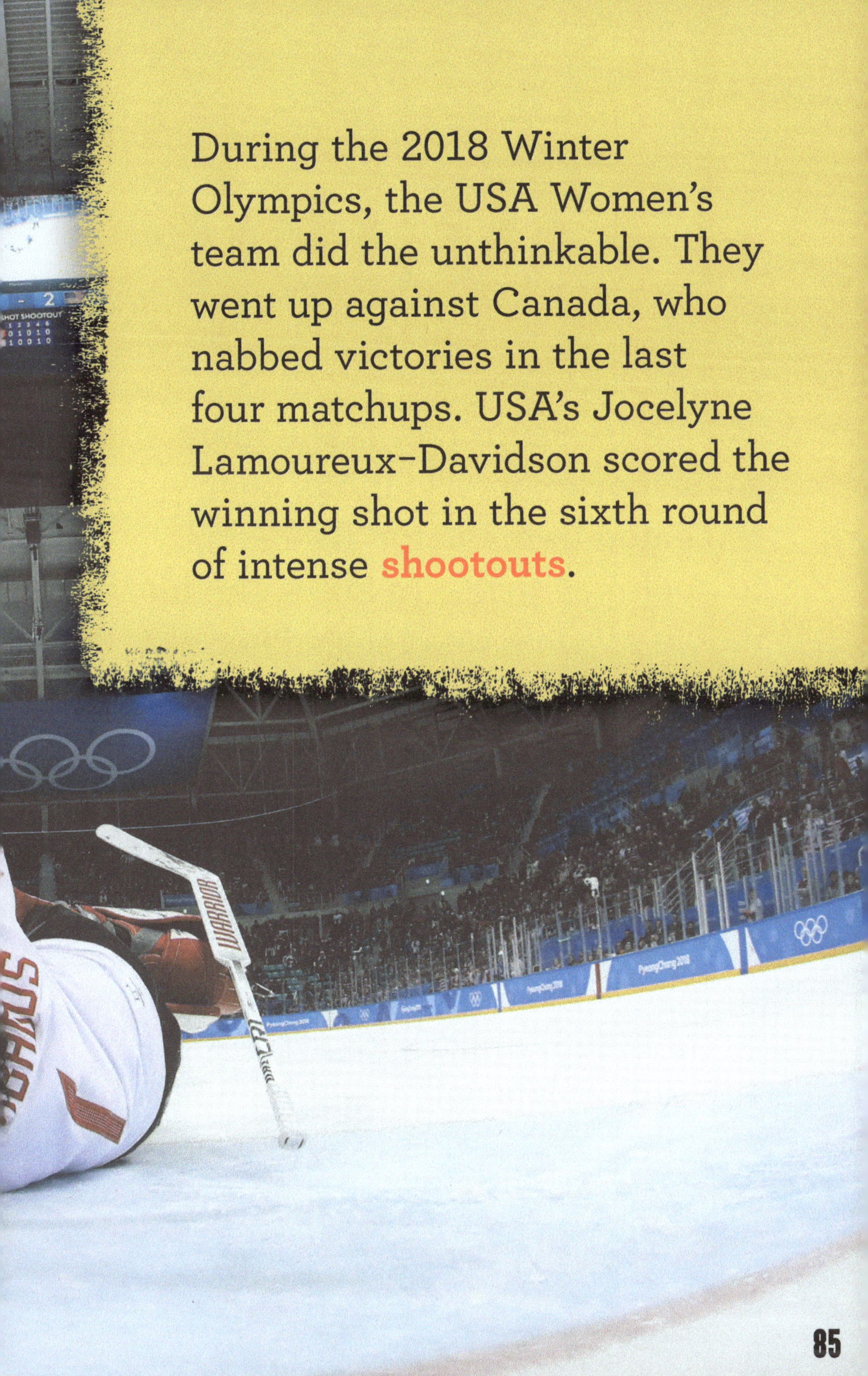

During the 2018 Winter Olympics, the USA Women's team did the unthinkable. They went up against Canada, who nabbed victories in the last four matchups. USA's Jocelyne Lamoureux-Davidson scored the winning shot in the sixth round of intense **shootouts**.

LEGACY

The "Miracle on Ice" made more than sports history. It has been recreated in made for TV movies to documentaries. In 2004, the hit movie *Miracle* was released on the big screen and starred Kurt Russell.

Fans of hockey watch for players to do the impossible on the ice, making it **breakaway** entertainment for all.

GLOSSARY

barn burner – a sporting event that is very intense and exciting.

breakaway – when a player has the puck and an open skating lane to the goal with no one in front of them.

overtime – additional minutes added to a tied-up game giving each team a chance to win.

shootout – in hockey, a tie-breaker method where 3 players from each team attempt a shot on the opponent's goalie. If the score remains tied, the shootout moves into a sudden death round.

Stanley Cup playoff – an elimination tournament played each year by qualifying teams in the NHL. The winner takes home the Stanley Cup trophy.

Soviets – the Soviet national ice hockey team that won nearly every world championship and Olympic tournament between 1954 and 1991.

MIRACLE MOMENTS IN
SOCCER
KENNY ABDO

TABLE OF CONTENTS

As the most-watched sport in the world, soccer reigns victorious over every other **pastime**.

Games similar to soccer were first recorded in China between the second and third centuries.

What we know as soccer today is believed to have started in mid-19th-century England.

Mind-blowing comebacks and wrong-footed victories have all carved themselves into soccer history.

97
GRIEZMAN

DO YOU BELIEVE?

Antonín Panenka made soccer history during the 1976 European finals. His **chip** won the **Championship** for Czechoslovakia in a **penalty shootout**. Defeating West Germany's harsh goalie, the 'Panenka Penalty' kick was born.

Diego Maradona scored the "Goal of the Century" minutes after his infamous "Hand of God" shot. He got the ball and ran 60 yards (55 m) in just 10 seconds to score! Argentina won the game.

Brandi Chastain made the game-winning goal for the USWNT in a **penalty shootout** against China. The 1999 Women's **World Cup** win was witnessed live by more than 90,000 fans and inspired generations to come.

It was not looking good for Liverpool during the 2005 **Champions League**. The team was down 0-3 against Milan. The Reds were able to tie it up within six minutes. Their win is considered one of the greatest comebacks in soccer history.

In 2016, Leicester City did more than break a very long losing streak. They overcame 5,000-to-one betting **odds** by winning the **Premier League**. The team was in last place with nine games to go. They ended up winning seven, **clinching** the **championship**.

LEGACY

Soccer is so popular that more than 3 billion people tuned in for the 2018 **World Cup**. Miracles on the soccer field have revealed how far teams and players will go to be the best. Which is a goal for everyone!

GROUD
TOLISSO
12
8

GLOSSARY

Champions League – a yearly club football (soccer) competition organized by the Union of European Football Associations.

championship – a game held to find a first-place winner.

chip – kicking the ball up into the air in a long arc.

clinch – to confirm a win.

odds – the calculated likelihood of a game's outcome.

pastime – an activity people participate in for their enjoyment.

penalty shootout – a method to determine a winner in a soccer match that cannot end in a tie, where 5 players from each team get one kick at the opponent's goal. The team that scores the most goals wins.

Premier League – the top level of the English Football (soccer) league system.

World Cup – an international soccer competition held every four years.

MIRACLE MOMENTS IN
TENNIS
KENNY ABDO

Photo Credits: AP Images, Granger Collection, Icon Sportswire, iStock, Newscom, Shutterstock
Production Contributors: Kenny Abdo, Jennie Forsberg, Grace Hansen
Design Contributors: Dorothy Toth, Neil Klinepier

TABLE OF CONTENTS

TENNIS

Even with so many other sports in the world, tennis is still considered an **ace** among them.

It is believed that tennis came from northern France in the 12th or 13th century. Then, a ball was hit with the palm of a hand. Major Walton Clopton Wingfield wrote the rules and patented the game in 1874.

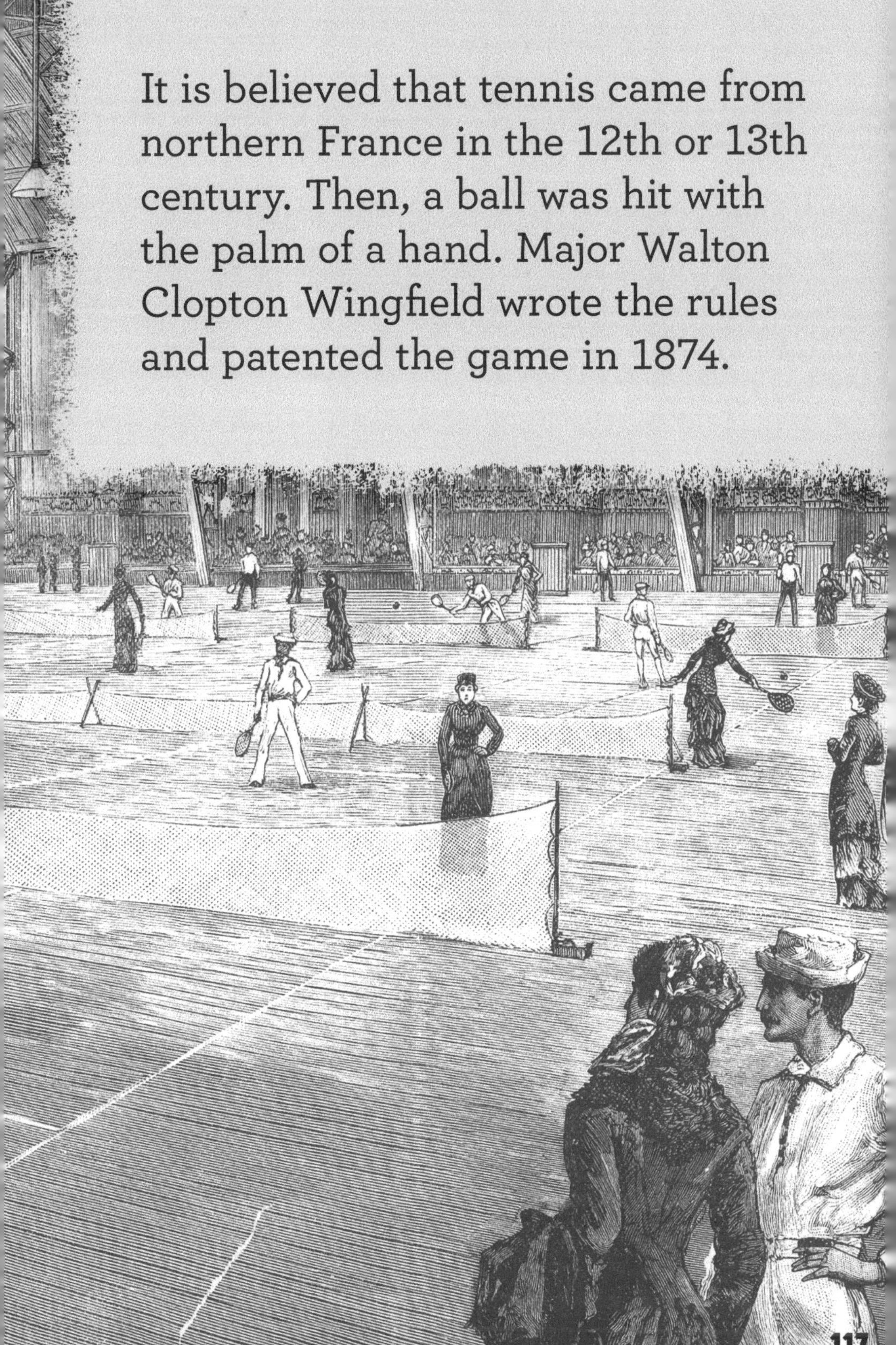

Everything from record-setting match lengths to hard-fought victories have graced the clay court.

DO YOU BELIEVE?

Bjorn Borg shocked the world at the 1980 **Wimbledon Championships**. Up against infamous John McEnroe, Borg won the **title** with a final backhand pass. It was a tie-break win that has become tennis legend.

During the 1985 **Wimbledon Championships**, unknown 17-year-old German Boris Becker beat all-star Kevin Curren. Becker was the youngest player to ever win the tournament. He said, "This is going to change tennis in Germany." And it did.

Ending 2006 at number 95 in the world, Serena Williams was down and out. Making it to the 2007 **Australian Open Grand Slam** finals, Williams stunned by taking down number one player Maria Sharapova. It is considered one of the finest Grand Slam performances of all time.

The 2010 Wimbledon Grand Slam saw John Isner and Nicholas Mahut play the longest-ever tennis match to date.

The game went on for three days! It was completed in 11 hours and 5 minutes.

Andy Murray made history at **Wimbledon** in 2013. He became the first British player to win since 1936. He was also the first Scotland born person to win a singles **title** since 1896!

ROYAL
MARSDEN
Cancer Charity
adidas
adidas

LEGACY

These tennis court miracles have been captured in time. Not with just **highlight reels** and books, but with movies and documentaries.

Tennis has dedicated athletes and fans who all agree that with this sport, "love" means more than just zero.

GLOSSARY

ace – a winning serve that the returner does not touch.

Australian Open – the first of the four most important yearly tennis tournaments.

Grand Slam – also known as the majors, are four of the most important yearly tennis events, which includes the US, Australian, and French Opens and Wimbledon Championship.

highlight reel – the best moments of a certain game or athlete compiled into one film.

title – a first-place position in a contest.

Wimbledon Championship – the oldest and most respected tennis tournament in the world.

HISTORY OF
BASEBALL
KENNY ABDO

TABLE OF CONTENTS

BASEBALL

Sliding into homes around the world, baseball is one of the most popular sports in the U.S. and around the world.

Baseball is played between two teams of nine players on an enclosed field. The objective is to score more runs than the opponent.

WARM UP

Bat-and-ball games have been around for a long time. No one knows when they were created. It is believed they were first played in the mid 1700s or early 1800s.

FENWAY PARK

Baseball became the "national pastime" of the United States in the mid-1850s. The oldest ballpark still in use is Fenway Park in Boston, Massachusetts. It opened in 1912. It is older than both the Jefferson and Lincoln Memorials.

THRILL
CHOW

Baseball is fun for all ages. The youngest pitcher in Major **League** Baseball (MLB) history is Joe Nuxhall. He was just 15 years old when he first played for the Cincinnati Reds. Derek Jeter was 40 when he became the oldest player to have more than two hits during an **All-Star Game**.

The first MLB game aired on television in 1939. It was a **doubleheader** between the Brooklyn Dodgers and the Cincinnati Reds. The Dodgers won, 6 to 1.

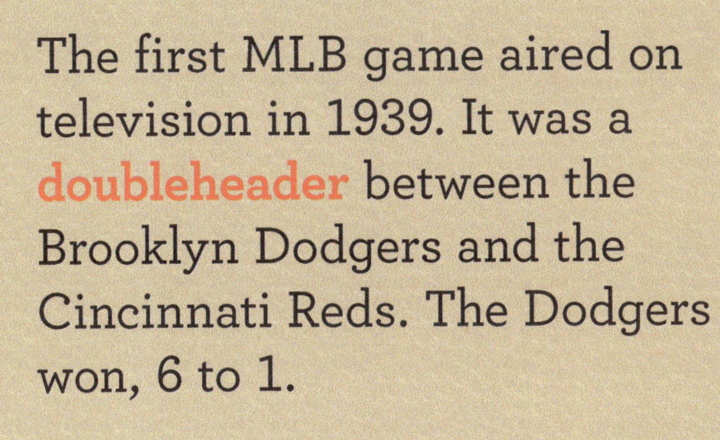

BIG SHOW

Baseball games will go as long as they need to. The longest was between the Milwaukee Brewers and the Chicago White Sox in 1984.

The game was called off after more than 8 hours of play across two days!

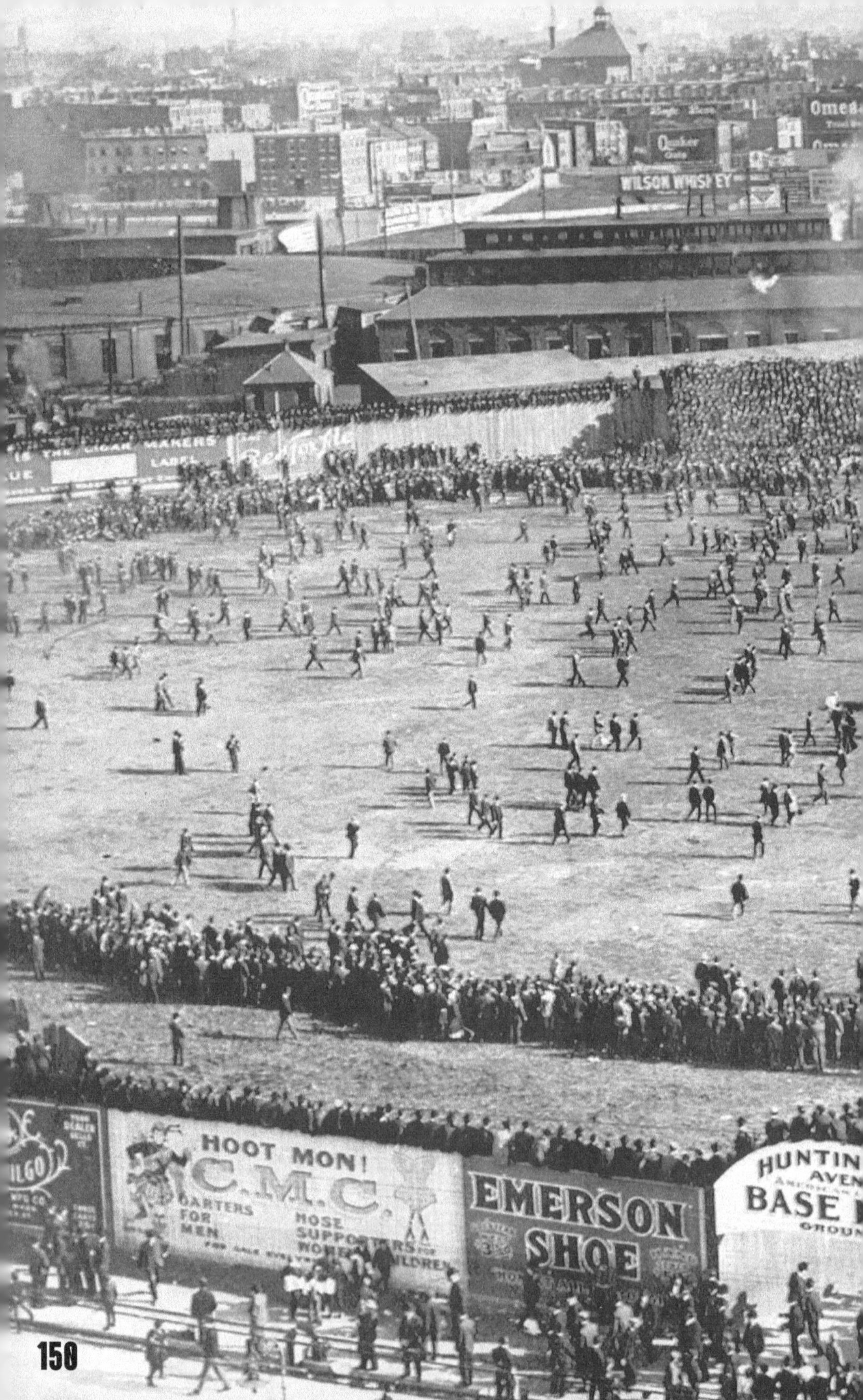
WILSON WHISKEY
CIGAR MAKERS
LABEL
HOOT MON!
C.M.C.
GARTERS FOR MEN
HOSE SUPPORTERS FOR
WOMEN CHILDREN
EMERSON SHOE
HUNTIN AVEN
BASE
GROU

The **World Series** is the **championship** series of the MLB that happens every year. A team from the American **League** (AL) and National League (NL) play in a best-of-seven playoff. The Boston Americans won the first World Series in 1903.

The Boston Red Sox beat the Los Angeles Dodgers in five games to win the 2018 **World Series**. The two teams played each other for the same **title** more than 100 years earlier. It is the longest gap between World Series meetings in MLB history.

GLOSSARY

All-Star Game – a yearly game played by the best players from the American (AL) and National league (NL).

championship – a game held to find a first-place winner.

doubleheader – two games played by the same teams back-to-back.

league – a group of teams that compete against each other.

opponent – a rival team.

title – a first-place position in a contest.

World Series – a series of games, where the team who wins a best-of-seven playoff is determined champions of the year.

History of

BASKETBALL

KENNY ABDO

TABLE OF CONTENTS

BASKETBALL

From packed arenas to driveways around the world, basketball puts the full-court press on every other sport.

Whether it is a college or pro game, the rules stay the same. **Dribble** the orange ball down the court and shoot it into your **opponent's** hoop.

WARM UP

Canadian physical education teacher James Naismith is credited for inventing basketball. On a rainy day in 1891, he looked for a way to keep his gym class busy. And so, the sport was born!

Peach baskets were originally used for basketball hoops. They were replaced by string nets in the early 1900s.

There were nine players on each basketball team at first. It was based on the number of players on a baseball team. Teams were later reduced to five players on the court.

The National Basketball **League** was created in 1937. The Basketball Association of America (BAA) was founded in 1946. They merged in 1976 to make the National Basketball Association (NBA).

The Women's National Basketball Association (WNBA) was formed 20 years later.

BIG SHOW

Wilt Chamberlain holds the NBA record for the most points scored in a single game. He alone racked up 100 points against the New York Knicks.

100

Phoenix Mercury's Diana Taurasi was voted the best woman basketball player of all time by ESPN in 2017. Her skills playing for UConn, the WNBA, Turkey, and Russia helped her clinch the title.

LeBron James is considered one of the best players in basketball history. He has led his team to the NBA **Finals** in every **season** between 2010 and 2018!

The Golden State Warriors were the 2018 NBA **Finals** champions. They beat the Cleveland Cavaliers in four out of four games. Warriors small forward Kevin Durant was named Most Valuable Player (MVP) averaging 28.8 points per game.

GLOSSARY

clinch – to confirm a win.

dribble – bouncing the ball on the floor to advance down the court.

Finals – the championship series of the NBA where the team who wins best-of-seven games is determined champions of the year.

league – a group of teams that compete against each other.

opponent – a rival team.

season – the portion of the year where certain games are played.

History of
FOOTBALL
PATRIOTS
KENNY ABDO

TABLE OF CONTENTS

FOOTBALL

Football scores big with fans from college games to pro bowls to fantasy **leagues**. With hundreds of years of history, the sport is one of the most popular in the world.

Football is played between two teams of 11 players. They play on a 100-yard long field that has goalposts on each end. Each team can score points in many ways. One team getting the ball into the other team's **end zone** is the main goal.

WARM UP

Football is believed to come from the English games **rugby** and soccer. American football was started by player and coach Walter Camp from Yale University.

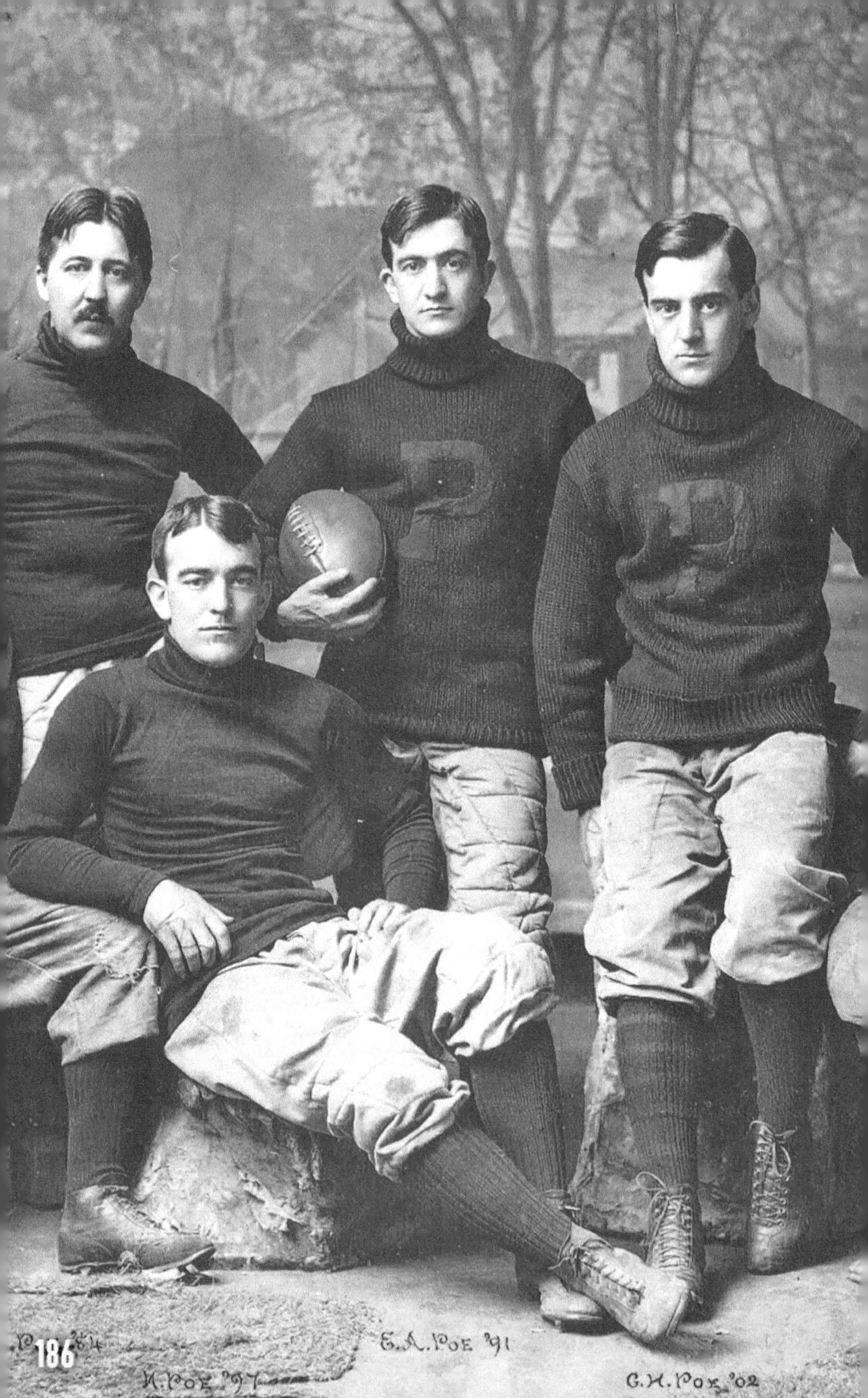
E. A. POE '91
N. POE '97
G. H. POE '02

The first game of football was played in 1869. Princeton University went up against Rutgers University. The rules were more like **rugby's** and the ball was round. Rutgers won the game, 6 to 4.

The National Football **League** (NFL) was created in 1920. The American Football League (AFL) was created 40 years later.

In 1967, the NFL and AFL decided to play against each other. It was called the AFL-NFL **Championship** Game or the **Super Bowl**.

In 1970, the AFL joined the NFL forming one **league**. Today, the **Super Bowl** is still played between the National Football Conference (NFC) and the American Football Conference (AFC).

The winning team of the **Super Bowl** gets the Vince Lombardi **trophy**. It is made of sterling silver and is valued at more than $25,000!

BIG SHOW

Washington Redskins quarterback Frank Filchock set a record in 1939. He threw a 99-yard pass to fullback Andy Farkas for a touchdown. Eli Manning matched the feat by tossing a 99-yard **bomb** to Victor Cruz in 2011.

In 2018, the Philadelphia Eagles beat the New England Patriots at Super Bowl LII. Eagles quarterback Nick Foles, who passed for 373 yards and three touchdowns, **clinched** the Most Valuable Player (MVP) award. He is the first player to ever throw and catch a touchdown pass at a Super Bowl!

12
58
WHITE
28

Tom Brady is considered one of the best players in NFL history. He has led the Patriots to the **Super Bowl** nine times! They beat the LA Rams in 2019, making it their sixth **championship** victory!

GLOSSARY

bomb – a long pass thrown to a receiver.

championship – a game held to find a first-place winner.

clinch – to confirm a win.

end zone – the area at the end of the field that the ball must enter to score a touchdown.

league – a group of teams that compete against each other.

rugby – a game played between two teams of 13 players. The ball can be kicked, carried, and passed from hand to hand to score a goal. Forward passing is not allowed.

Super Bowl – the NFL championship game played once a year.

trophy – an object you receive as a prize for winning during a game or event.

HISTORY OF
GOLF
KENNY ABDO

Photo Credits: Alamy, AP Images, Granger Collection, Icon Sportswire, iStock, Shutterstock
Production Contributors: Kenny Abdo, Jennie Forsberg, Grace Hansen
Design Contributors: Dorothy Toth, Neil Klinepier

TABLE OF CONTENTS

GOLF

Teeing off in the 1400s, golf has withstood the test of time and has become a major sport throughout the world!

Golf is played on a course that usually has 18 holes. Players use a variety of **clubs** to get their golf balls into each hole in as few **strokes** as possible.

WARM UP

Modern day golf is traced back to Scotland in the mid-1400s. The sport was banned by the Scottish government because they thought it interfered with military training.

The first golf balls were made of feathers wrapped in leather. Wood balls were in use by the mid-1800s. Instead of **tees**, golfers would hit the ball from a mound of sand.

There are four major golf tournaments. They are the Masters, the US Open, the Open **Championship**, and the PGA Championship. Golfers from around the world play to prove who the best really is.

ANNUAL
CHAMPIONSHIP
OF THE
PROFESSIONAL
GOLFERS
ASSOCIATION
OF
AMERICA
RODMAN WANAMAKER
TROPHY

The first PGA **Championship** was played in 1916. Jim Barnes walked away with $500 and a diamond-studded gold medal. The first Women's PGA Championship was played in 1955. Beverly Hanson **clinched** the **title** and earned $1,200.

TITLEHOLDERS
CHAMPION

BIG SHOW

Park Sung-hyun was named the best golfer by the Women's World Golf Rankings in 2017. She won the Women's PGA **Championship** in 2018.

Hana
Financial Group
work

Brooks Koepka is a rising star in the world of professional golf. Koepka is one of only five players in the history of golf to win the US Open and PGA **Championship** in the same year!

Tiger Woods has been called the greatest golfer to ever walk the **links**. He hit his first **hole-in-one** when he was just eight years old! Woods has won more than 80 PGA events, including the 2019 Masters!

GLOSSARY

championship – a game held to find a first-place winner.

clinch – to confirm a win.

club – a slender shaft with a wood or iron head that is used for hitting the golf ball. They come in different sizes to hit the ball different distances.

hole-in-one – a shot in golf that enters the hole from the tee with no other shots in between.

links – another term for a golf course.

stroke – hitting or attempting to hit the golf ball as one point.

tee – a small wooden peg where the golf ball is set to be hit.

tee off – to begin a round or a single hole of golf.

title – a first-place position in a contest.

HISTORY OF
GYMNASTICS
KENNY ABDO

TABLE OF CONTENTS

GYMNASTICS

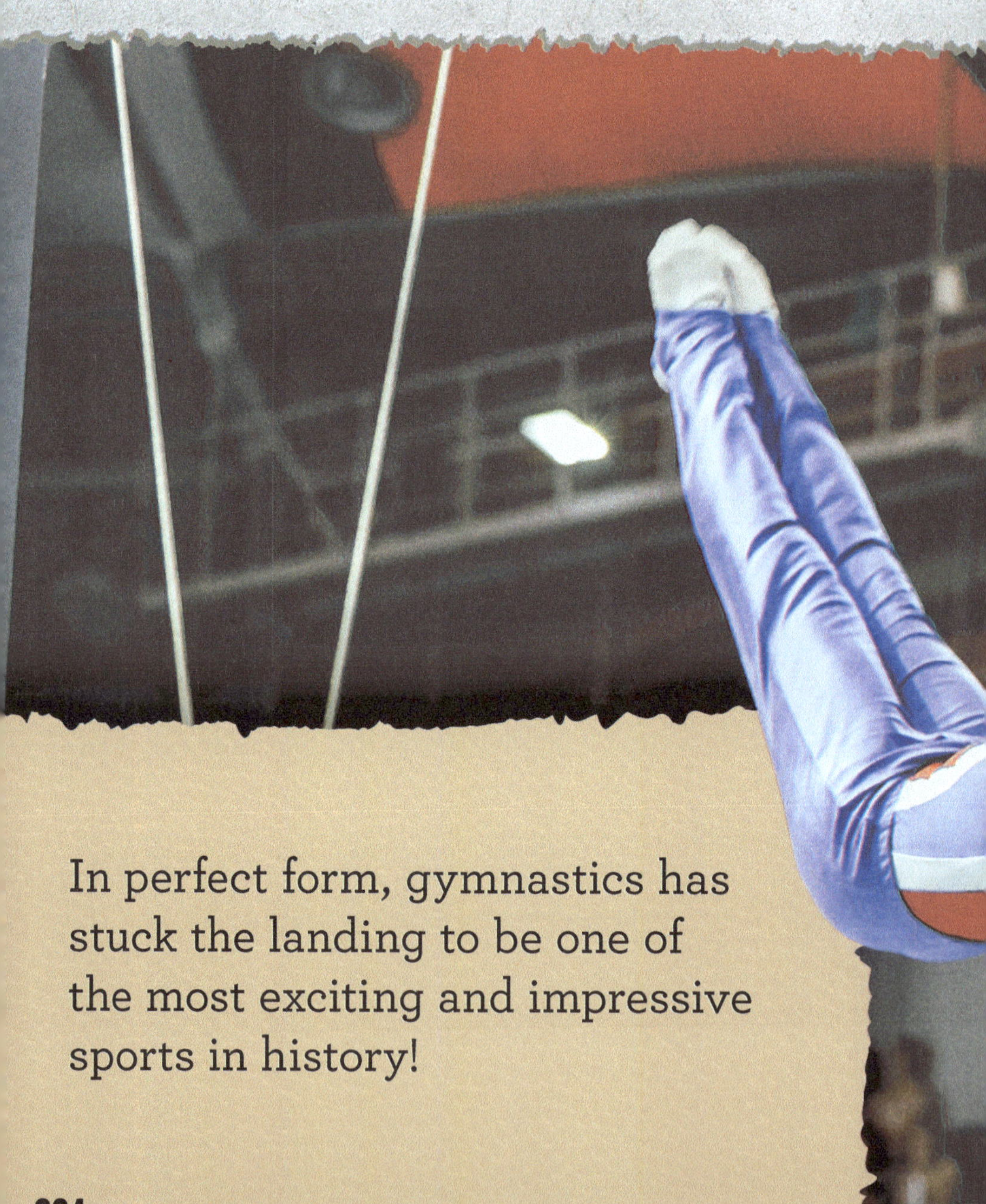

In perfect form, gymnastics has stuck the landing to be one of the most exciting and impressive sports in history!

Gymnastics is broken up into many **disciplines**. Each one tests the gymnast's strength, agility, and balance. All events are scored from 0 to 10 points.

WARM UP

Gymnastics is believed to have started long ago in ancient Greece. It was supposed to help the body develop. After the Romans conquered Greece, they made gymnastics a formal sport. It was also practiced for warfare.

230

Fredrich Ludwig Jahn was a physical education teacher in Berlin. In 1809, he invented the parallel bars, the balance beam, and the rings for his students. Jahn is known as the "father of gymnastics."

The International Gymnastics Federation (FIG) was created in 1881. It is the **governing** body of the sport. FIG sets the rules for judging gymnastic skills. This is known as the Code of Points.

The first **Olympic** games were held in 1896. Men's gymnastics has been a part of the games since then. The first women's event was in 1928. Romania's Nadia Comăneci scored the first perfect 10 in 1976.

BIG SHOW

American Gymnast Mary Lou Retton made history at the 1984 **Olympics**. She was the first American woman to win the **all-around** gold medal. Retton's skills made her the most popular athlete in the world!

LONGINES
Rotterdam
city of sports

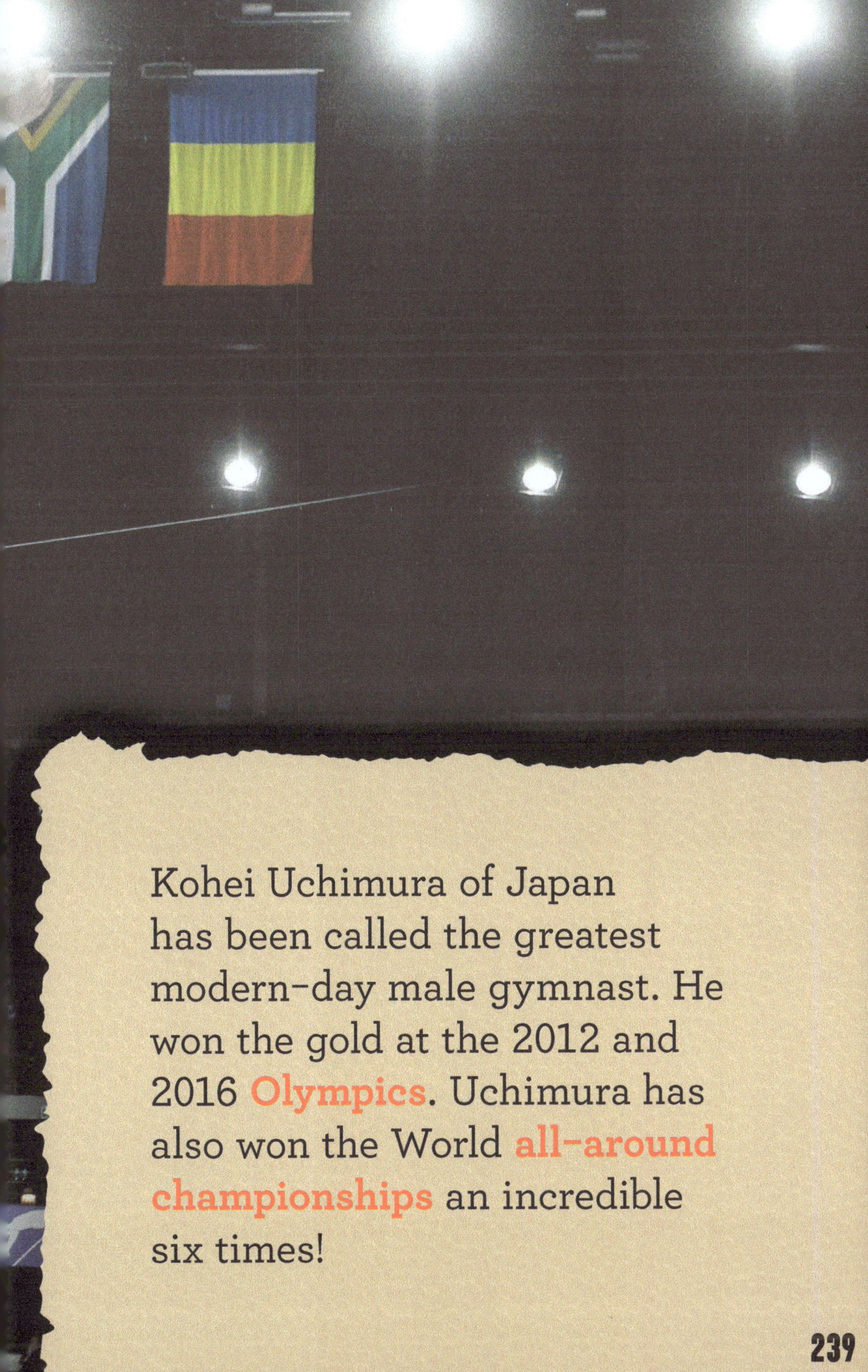

Kohei Uchimura of Japan has been called the greatest modern-day male gymnast. He won the gold at the 2012 and 2016 **Olympics**. Uchimura has also won the World **all-around championships** an incredible six times!

Simone Biles of the USA won an amazing six medals at the 2018 World Gymnastics **Championships**. She has earned 20 medals overall, the most by any female gymnast.

GLOSSARY

all-around – a gymnastics event where the scores of each exercise is totaled up to decide the winner.

championship – a game held to find a first-place winner.

conquer – to victoriously take by force.

discipline – a branch of gymnastics learned through strict practice and exercise.

govern – to enforce the rules and laws.

Olympics – the biggest sporting event in the world that is divided into summer and winter games.

warfare – fighting between differing militaries.

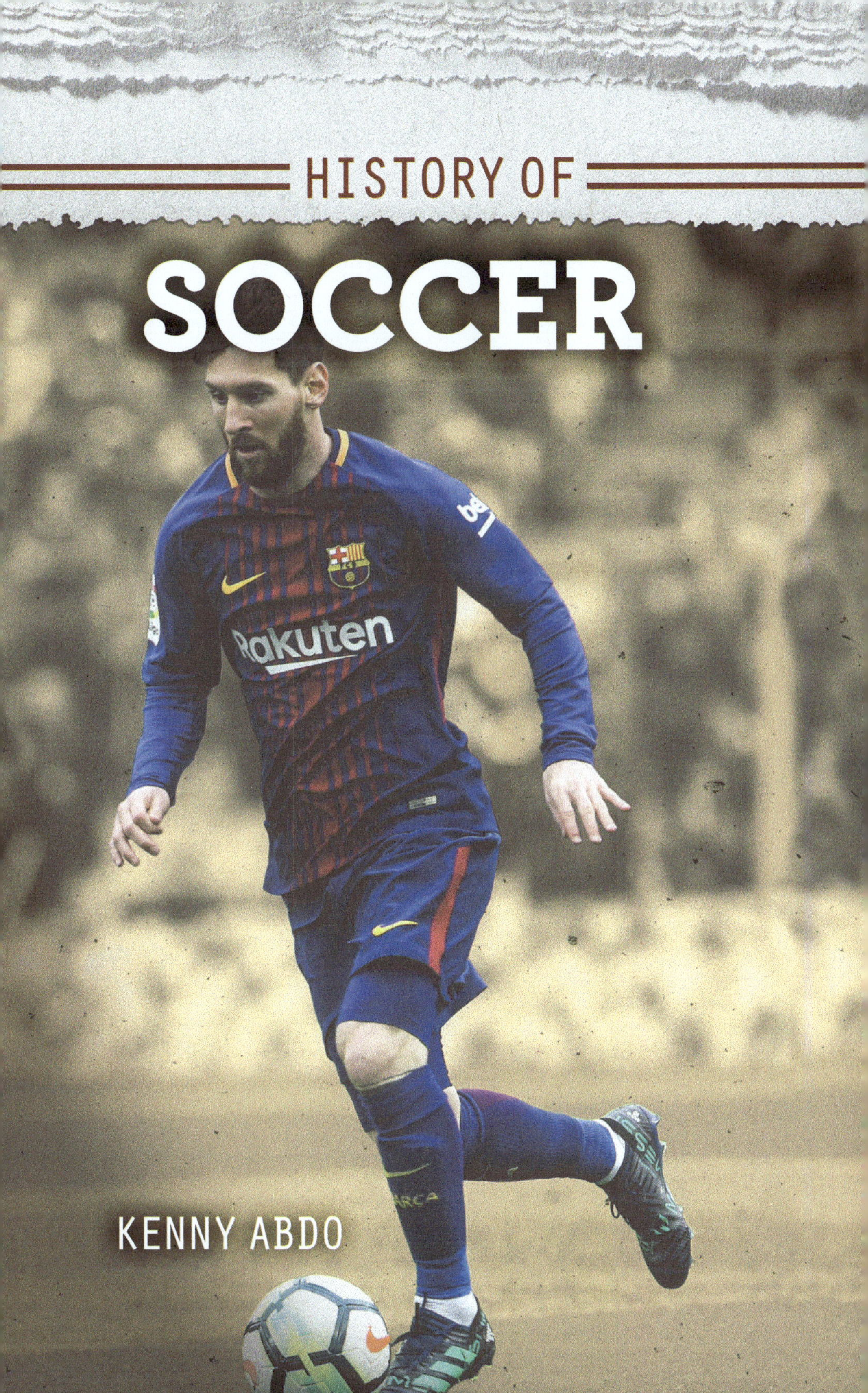

HISTORY OF
SOCCER
KENNY ABDO

TABLE OF CONTENTS

SOCCER

Soccer has been played by everyone, from kids to pros, throughout the **centuries**. With more than 3 billion people watching the 2018 **World Cup**, soccer is the most beloved sport in the entire world.

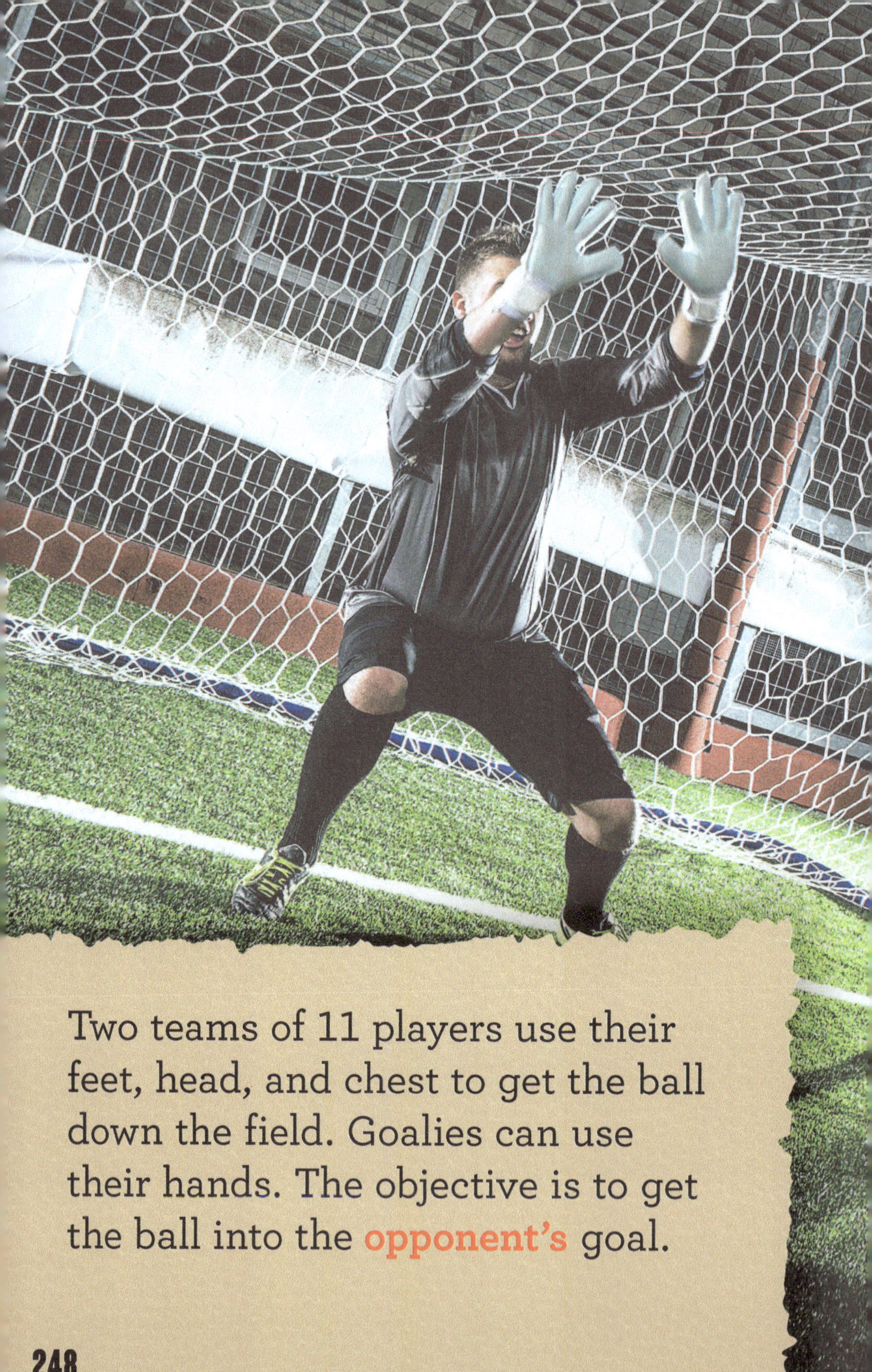

Two teams of 11 players use their feet, head, and chest to get the ball down the field. Goalies can use their hands. The objective is to get the ball into the opponent's goal.

WARM UP

There have been many games like soccer throughout history. Historians think that the first form of soccer was played by the Chinese in the 2nd and 3rd **centuries**.

Later, the game spread to countries like Japan, Greece, and Australia. Modern soccer was first played in 1863 in England. It was then that the Football Association was created. It was the first official **governing** body of soccer.

The International Federation of Association Football (FIFA) was formed in 1904. They organize the major soccer **tournaments** around the world.

The biggest **tournament** is the FIFA **World Cup**. It is played every four years. The first one was held in Uruguay in 1930. The first Women's World Cup was played in China in 1991.

BIG SHOW

Brazilian soccer player Pelé is considered one of the greatest of all time. He was the youngest player to ever play in a **World Cup** at 17 years old. Pelé also **scored** an amazing 1,281 goals in his career!

PRESIDENTE
CINZA

Marta Vieira da Silva was voted the Best Women's player of 2018 by FIFA. She holds the Women's World Cup top-score record with 15 goals. Marta led the Brazilian national team to win the silver medal at both the 2004 and 2008 Summer Olympics.

Lionel Messi is thought to be the best player on the field today. He has fought his way to the **World Cup** an incredible 18 times. Through 2018, Messi had won the **European Golden Shoe** award a record five times!

GLOSSARY

century – an era of 100 years.

European Golden Shoe – an award given to the leading goalscorer of the season.

govern – to enforce the rules and laws.

Olympics – the biggest sporting event in the world that is divided into summer and winter games.

opponent – a rival team.

score – a collection of points to determine the winner and loser of a game.

tournament – a series of games played for a championship.

World Cup – an international soccer competition held every four years.